SEASIDE POSTCARD

A Comedy

TERENCE FRISBY

SAMUEL   FRENCH

LONDON

NEW YORK   TORONTO   SYDNEY   HOLLYWOOD

SEASIDE POSTCARD

First presented by the Young Vic Company at The Cut, London S.E.1, on the 18th November 1977, with the following cast of characters:

Man	Teddy Green
Girl	Suzannah Williams
Sharon Spicer	Vicky Ogden
Terry Rees	C. J. Allen
Glynis Spicer	Judy Wilson
Shirley Thompson	Rosalind Boxall
Martin Spicer	Ian Taylor
Leslie Thompson	Peter O'Farrell

The Play directed by the Author
Setting by Mark Wheeler

The action takes place on a beach in North Cornwall

The setting used for the Young Vic production was a simple area of sand with an enormous seaside postcard as backing

Time—the present

Please note our NEW ADDRESS:

Samuel French Ltd
52 Fitzroy Street London W1P 6JR
Tel: 01 - 387 9373

SEASIDE POSTCARD

A beach in North Cornwall

Seaside sounds are heard—a lighthouse foghorn, seagulls, waves, distant shouts

A respectable-looking man, possibly of military appearance, wanders on with binoculars round his neck. He looks about him, stretches, then peers through his binoculars across the audience. He sees what he is looking for, namely an attractive female shape and leaps into a pointing posture letting out a groan of pleasure. He follows its movements across the back of the auditorium then lowers his binoculars and gives another little groan of contentment. He sees someone coming, gives another groan, more anticipatory this time, and drops out of sight

A pretty Girl with a nice figure enters. She looks about her then selects a place. She drops her things then wriggles gently and sensually out of her clothes. She is wearing a bikini underneath. The Man reappears. As she wriggles out of her jeans, the man lets out a groan which is followed by the lighthouse foghorn. The Girl considers removing her bikini top. As she puts her hands up to remove it the man gives a squeak of pleasure which is followed by a seagull squawk. The Girl looks round as the man dives for cover. She changes her mind about sunbathing topless. She stretches, feels the warm sun, then with a final luxurious, narcissistic movement lies full length. Pause. Sound effect of a seagull swooping. A sizeable dollop of seagull dropping smacks her squarely amidships. She sits up with a jerk and looks at her bespattered stomach

Girl Ooouargh!

She gathers her things and quickly leaves in angry discomfort, looking for something to wipe herself clean. The Man is furious. He shakes his fist at the sky

Man Bloody seagulls! (*He peers off through his binoculars after the girl. He groans with ecstasy*) Oh, look at her move. Like two ferrets in a sack. (*He throws back his head and lets out an uninhibited yell of enjoyed frustrated lust, as he dances with glee.*

He pulls himself soberly together then sees another person approaching)

The Man hides and exits. Sharon Spicer enters. She has large and wonderful breasts. Her every move is designed to entice and excite the man she wants, Terry Rees, who follows her on. He, poor sap, is besotted. He looks back and satisfied comes near to her. She is posed staring out over the audience. She sighs

Sharon Oooh! It's lovely, innit?

Terry edges closer

Look at that ship out there.

Terry gets behind her

Terry Where?
Sharon (*pointing*) There.

He puts his hands on her waist. She leans into him. He would like to raise his hands to her breasts but dare not.

Terry Oh, yeah.
Sharon Like a toy one.
Terry Yeah.
Sharon And the lighthouse too. Triffic innit?
Terry Amazing.
Sharon (*wriggling*) Standing up out there, all straight and proud with the sea surging about.
Terry I know how it feels.
Sharon 'S lovely, innit.

They slide smoothly into a romantic kiss. He puts in plenty of head work and runs his hands up and down her

The Man reappears at a new vantage point, watching through binoculars

(*Breaking*) Phaw. Terry Rees, you dunnalf know how to kiss.
Terry I know.

He tries again. She breaks

Sharon No, the others are coming.
Terry They're miles behind.
Sharon They'll see us.

Terry No, they can't. We're hidden.
Sharon All right, then. One quickie.

Another kiss of simulated passion. Sharon turns herself so that her back is to him and sighs and stares romantically out to sea. Terry finally plucks up courage to raise his hand and cover her breast. He sighs audibly with pleasure. She allows him a few seconds of this before thrusting him sharply away with her behind. Terry's sigh turns to a yelp of pain

    Stop it.
Terry Why?
Sharon I don't like it.
Terry You do.
Sharon I don't.
Terry Well I do.
Sharon I know you do. You're always feeling my boobs.
Terry I like 'em.
Sharon I dunno what you see in 'em.
Terry They're lovely. Better'n that bleeding lighthouse.
Sharon (*pleased*) Honest?
Terry Yeah.
Sharon You only want me for one thing.
Terry Two (*He grins shyly*)
Sharon See.
Terry Anyway. I don't. I want you for—well—just for you. I want you for everything.
Sharon Oh, yeah, *now*. Then when you got it—slam, bam, thank you ma'am.
Terry No, no, honest.
Sharon You won't respect me as a person.
Terry I do respect you as a person.
Sharon You don't.
Terry I do.
Sharon Do you?
Terry Yeah. I respect you like mad.
Sharon Yeah, now. But you won't after.
Terry I will after. I'll respect you more as a person.
Sharon Will you?
Terry Yeah.
Sharon Course, it'd be different if . . .

Terry What?

Sharon If we was engaged. Oo, look at that bird up there. Innit unusual. What is it?

Terry A seagull.

Sharon Oh.

Terry You look beautiful like that.

Sharon Ha.

Terry You always look beautiful.

Sharon I'll bet you say that to all the girls.

Terry No, no, you are. Really beautiful. Not just pretty, but beautiful.

Sharon So are you.

Terry Ah, come on, you're just being silly.

Sharon No, I'm not. I mean you're not handsome or anything, but you are beautiful. I mean your character.

Terry I'm not.

Sharon You are.

Terry Attractive.

Sharon What?

Terry That's what I am. Attractive. No more. I mean some people have got it, and some haven't. Let's sit over here.

Sharon Oh.

Terry There's nothing in that. We gotta sit somewhere, 'less you're thinking of walking all day.

He sits. She sits away from him

Terry Over here.

Sharon No.

Terry Don't be mean.

Sharon No.

Terry Go on.

Sharon No.

Terry They'll be here soon.

Sharon Well, you'd better come here then or you'll be too late.

He skuttles over and, horizontal, they kiss again. Terry rolls over on top of her and gets one knee in between hers. The Man groans. Again she allows this for a moment then decides his time is up. She knees him. He gasps and breaks away

Terry Ooh. What d'you do that for?

Sharon You know what for.

Terry You could've hurt me.

Sharon That was the idea.

Terry I mean damaged me.

Sharon Some hopes. You should control yourself.

Terry I'm only human.

Sharon So was Jack the Ripper.

Terry Coh, 'blige me, Sharon. You'n half mean with it.

Sharon Well, why don't you try talking to me for a change, 'stead of trying to screw me all the time.

Terry I do talk to you. I talked to you last night. For hours. I nearly lost me voice shouting against the waves. You fell asleep.

Sharon 'S the sea air. You soon woke me up though, din ya. Blinking hands everywhere.

Terry You gonna come down the Lobster Pot disco again tonight?

Sharon Dunno.

Terry Oh, go on.

Sharon I'll see.

Terry Don't then, I don't care. (*He rolls over away from her*)

Sharon They got an old Elvis film on down the Rex in Padstow.

Terry He's a twat.

Sharon Oo, may your tongue drop out. You shouldn't speak ill of the dead.

Terry I'm gonna watch the best of Morecambe and Wise on telly then I'm going down the Lobster Pot disco. You can take your rotten, smelly boobs and wave 'em at Elvis and I hope he waves something back.

She is outraged

Sharon Terry Rees. You dirty devil!

Glynis Spicer enters and sees Sharon and Terry

Glynis Oh, there you are, little love birds. Found you at last. Oo, what a drag through them sand dunes, like walking on cornflakes. It's wrecked my new wedge heels. (*Glynis waves and calls off*) Whoo-oo.

There is an incoherent, agonized female shout in answer

They're over here.

More noise from the female, off, which continues as Glynis shouts

Yes, over here. Come on 's lovely over here. Lovely little hollow.
(*To Terry and Sharon*) Lovely here innit? (*Archly*) You found
yourself a nice sheltered little place didn't you? (*To Sharon*)
Can't trust you out of my sight can I? (*To Terry*) Dunno what
it is about you, Terry, but ever since you came along she's been
a changed girl. Sort of—awakened. Just as well I can trust *you*
innit?

Terry reacts

Oo, look! Look at that little ship out there. Innit lovely. And
that lighthouse. Oo-er. Reminds me of something. Now, what
was it? (*She shades her eyes and stares out*)

Terry I'm sorry, Sharon, honest.

*Martin Spicer and Shirley Thompson stagger on, weighed down
with things for the beach. Martin stands, loaded, like a weary
mule*

Glynis Oh, there you are at last. Look at this lovely little hollow
they've found, naughty things. Just what we were looking for.

Shirley Oh, thank goodness. I'm ready to drop.

Glynis Oh, Shirley really, you shouldn't carry all those things.

Shirley I don't mind.

Glynis What's happened to your Leslie?

Shirley He's gone off into the sand dunes for a minute.

Glynis Oh, really. They're so thoughtless, men. No consideration.

Shirley Well he had to go. He couldn't help it.

Glynis Hm. Yes. Any excuse.

Shirley It's all that beer at breakfast.

Glynis Hm.

Shirley Well, he *is* on holiday.

Glynis You should have asked me to help you carry something.

Shirley No, no, it's all right. We don't want you straining your
back again. It's not worth it. (*She drops everything and sags*)

Glynis No, you're probably right. Oo, I say. Look over here.
Here's another lovely little hollow. All sheltered.

Shirley Yes, there's lots of 'em. You slide down one side then scramble up the other, then down, then up, then . . .

Glynis I think this one's even nicer than that one.

Shirley This one's very nice, Glynis.

Glynis You get an even better view of the lighthouse.

Shirley I can see it quite well from here.

Glynis And it's more sheltered from the wind.

Shirley Oh, well. (*She picks up the things she has just put down*)

Sharon They're all exactly the same, Mum.

Glynis No, no, they're not. There's a subtle difference we'll notice after we've been sat down for a while.

Shirley I'm sure your mother knows best, Sharon. Come on.

Sharon Oo-oh.

Glynis I'm sure I'm only thinking of everybody's comfort.

Sharon Of course you are.

Glynis Here let me carry something. (*She picks up a small article*)

Terry There's a lovely little hollow just back that way, Mrs Spicer. All private.

Glynis Oh, really?

Terry Yes, the best of all of 'em. We sort of fell into it.

Glynis Well, why didn't you stop there then, Terry, dear.

Terry There was two people at it in there.

The Man lets out a joyous exclamation and quickly exits

Sharon That's all you think about. Anyway they weren't at it. They was only . . .

Glynis Spare us the details, Sharon dear. I don't think we want to join them.

Shirley They looked well joined already when I passed.

Glynis Well are you all coming or not. Martin, bring those things over here will you, and put 'em down—er—no—um . . .

Shirley Come on, kids. Let's have a quiet life.

Leslie enters

Leslie Hallo, oh yes. Lovely spot, this. Who found it?

Terry We did.

Leslie Smashing. 'Ere, there's a couple in a hollow over there at it like knives.

Shirley We know, dear. Don't draw attention.

Leslie *You* know. All the beach knows. I ain't seen so many binoculars since Derby day.

Shirley Perhaps they're bird-watching.

Leslie We'll be as snug as bugs in a rug here. Whah, it's baking hot innit, I hope you kept that beer cool, love.

Shirley We're going into the next hollow, Leslie. It's nicer.

Leslie But this is perfect.

Sharon Mum likes that one better.

Leslie sighs audibly

Shirley Yes, Mrs—um—Glynis thinks we'll be more comfortable there.

Leslie Does she? What does her husband think?

Martin I don't mind.

Leslie and Glynis play a grim game of exaggerated charm and politeness

Leslie I think that one'll lose the sun earlier.

Glynis I don't think so.

Leslie Yes, you see it's the angle of it, you see. It's angled away from the south. (*He points*)

Glynis Away from . . .? Well, that's the sea, innit?

Leslie Yes.

Glynis So that's west. The sun's there now—(*she points at it*)—and it'll set there, so how . . .?

Leslie Ah, but that's not west. (*He points*)

Glynis Well, this is Cornwall, innit. And Cornwall's in the West of England and *there's*—(*she points*)—the sea so *that* must be west.

Leslie Ah, but we're on the north coast of Cornwall. The sun sets over there. (*He points elsewhere*)

Sharon In that case we ought to find a hollow pointing that way. (*She points in another direction*)

Glynis No, no, the sun sets in the sea. We watched it from the caravan site yesterday.

Leslie Ah, but that was in our bay. It points in a different direction.

Glynis's veneer is wearing very thin

Glynis We watched the sun set in the sea, yesterday. Didn't we watch the sun set in the sea yesterday, Martin?

Martin There wasn't any sun yesterday.

Glynis Yes, there was. It came out for a minute and then set *in the sea*.

Martin Oh, yes. Then it rained.

Terry Actually this bay points east. (*He points*)

Leslie How can it point east?

Terry It does. The coast bends round. Anyway, look at my watch.

Leslie How's your bloody watch tell you which direction you're pointing?

Terry Simple. You do a sum. You point the hour hand at the sun then halve the angle between where the hour hand is now and twleve o'clock and that gives you south. There.

Glynis I don't think you can do that, Terry.

Terry Yes, you can. Look.

Glynis What about watches not made in this country?

Terry I learned it in Boy Scouts.

Leslie That was years ago.

Terry Look. I'll show you. It's nearly twelve o'clock so the little hand is pointing at the sun.

Glynis In that case the sun should be overhead if it's twelve o'clock.

Terry No, that's only in the Sahara. Not in Cornwall. The sun should be due south. So. There. See? So that's east. Logic.

Shirley Well. Isn't that clever. Isn't he clever, Sharon? You'll never get lost with him.

Sharon I wish he'd get lost now.

Terry What've I done?

Sharon What d'you want to argue with Mum for?

Terry I wasn't. I was arguing with him.

Sharon You was arguing with Mum.

Terry Well they was both wrong.

Shirley Well, maybe we should find somewhere else then. I should think that couple have finished by now.

Glynis Well, are you coming or not?

Leslie I know. Let Martin have the casting vote.

Martin Eh?

Leslie And there's no getting out of it by just agreeing with your missus.

Martin Well.

Glynis If he can't agree with me, how can he have the casting vote?

Martin I don't mind.

Sharon Oh, come on. Let's sit *somewhere*.

Shirley Yes, come on. Over there with Glynis. I'm sure it's beautiful.

Leslie Well, I don't care if it's Changri—bloody—La. I'm staying here. (*He sits*)

Terry Is that what you call democracy, Mr Thompson?

Shirley Well then, shall we stay . . .?

Glynis Oh, yes, here's nice enough, I suppose. If it's important to Leslie. Must keep our menfolk happy, eh, Shirley?

Shirley Oh, yes. (*She starts to get into a mess with her deck-chair*)

Glynis Well, come on, Martin. Put them things down.

Martin Here?

Glynis Of course here. Where else d'you think?

Martin You're sure.

Glynis Yes, positive. We took a vote.

Martin starts to unload

Leslie (*to Terry*) Anyway, what about British Summer Time?

Martin freezes

Terry What?

Leslie It's an hour out. That buggers up your calculations.

Terry I allowed for it. (*He did not*)

They start to settle. Martin moves last

Shirley Well, isn't this lovely. All peaceful.

Glynis Oh, yes. I'm so looking forward to soaking up a bit of sun. I'll have my chaise just here, I think, Martin. No-o. Now let's see . . .

Leslie Where's that beer, dear?

Shirley Here you are. In the cold bag.

Leslie Here, d'you hear that? Where's that beer, dear. I'm a poet and don't know it. (*He laughs*)

Martin (*joining in*) Yes. Then you said, "Here, d'you hear that?"

Leslie What?

Martin You said, "Where's that beer, dear" . . .

Leslie I know I did. I just said I said it.

Martin Then you said, "Here, d'you hear that?" You're a poet and don't know it squared.

Leslie Pardon?

Terry Then he just said said twice.

Martin Eh?

Terry He said, "I said I said it."

Sharon So have you.

Terry Pardon.

Sharon You've just said said twice too.

Leslie He said it three times.

Martin Twice two's four.

Leslie Listen, I was only asking for a beer.

Martin makes a dismal attempt at campness. Terry and Leslie join in

Martin A dear beer or a beer, dear.

Terry I'll have a cheap one, sweetie.

Leslie (*to Martin*) What about you, my love?

Martin Oh, ta. I'd like a medium one with lots of spirit. Get it? Medium? Spirit? (*He laughs*)

Glynis I don't know about drinking beer. I can't understand 'em sober.

Leslie O.K.? Lager or light ale?

Glynis I'm sure he'd love a half of something when he's finished.

Leslie Eh?

Glynis Getting us all settled.

Martin In a minute thank you, Leslie. In a while I'll have a light ile. (*He sniggers*)

Glynis Oh, really.

Martin Sorry, dear.

Martin blows up a lilo

Leslie I should think so. You're not out here to enjoy yourself.

Shirley We got some nice Spanish Sauternes for the ladies.

Glynis Well, I don't know if I should.

Shirley And then there's some nice bits of cold chicken, French bread sandwiches . . .

Leslie You got my peanut butter?

Shirley Yes, and bacon-flavoured crisps, some fruit —

Leslie (*holding it up*) And for after, a good swig of cherry brandy for the ladies . . .

Shirley Oo, we'll all be tiddly.

Leslie And three-star cognac for the men.

Glynis Well, I don't know. I don't know if we should with the sun on us.

Sharon What difference does the sun make?

Glynis Oh, you can't drink the hard stuff in the sun. That has terrible effects. They never did in the tropics.

Sharon Who?

Glynis Anyone. The Empire builders. Haven't you ever heard of sundowners? The sundowner was the first one of the day. That was when they could start.

Sharon I never knew that.

Glynis No, well. There you are. You children don't learn these things now there's no Empire.

Shirley Amazing what we've lost really, isn't it.

Martin I was out there you know.

Leslie Where?

Martin In the Empire. Kenya. When I was a conscript. They had Mau-Mau everywhere then. People being killed. Horrible deaths. Hands and arms and all their bits and pieces chopped off.

Shirley Who wants a chicken leg?

Martin I was very happy in Kenya.

Terry I thought Mau-Mau was an illness, like beriberi.

Leslie No, they was a secret society. Only now they're the government.

Shirley Yeah, well they all start like that, don't they.

Leslie Oh, well, who's gonna be first to get a tanned behind? Wey-hey. (*He drops his trousers and strikes a pose. On the seat of his underpants is the legend "Who's a cheeky boy, then?"*)

Shirley You, obviously.

Leslie Come on, then. Get 'em off, everybody! Last one stripped's a ninny.

Leslie's last remark is almost a challenge to Martin, who immediately drops his trousers. As Leslie hunts for his bathers in a bag, Glynis glares at Martin, who wraps his lilo round his middle and shuffles to a bag to get his bathers. As he passes her, Shirley takes off her trousers to reveal on the seat of her knickers "There's a tiger in my tank". They all get undressed and into bathing-costumes, discreetly hiding themselves from each other with towels. In spite of the fact that they all, with the exception of Sharon, take off everything to get into their bathing costumes it is a period of utter propriety. They hide under towels and indulge to the full the English habits of public undressing; red-faced wriggles, furtive looks, nervous clutches at clothing that might fall to reveal any forbidden parts of the body. Amid the general air of shame there is an embarrassed air of concentration on oneself that seems to imply that no-one else is present.

All of them put towels round themselves and remove the bottom half of their clothes. Leslie while hiding himself tries to see what he can of the others, particularly Sharon. Sharon reacts and moves away and as Leslie tries to get a look at her Terry puts himself between them. Glynis has got in a mess with her knickers caught round one ankle and is trying to free them with her other foot as she holds a towel round herself. Sharon gets into difficulties wriggling out of her tight trousers or jeans under her towel

Glynis Sharon, take your trousers off first, then put your towel round you.

Sharon shakes her head

(*Affronted*) Sharon.
Sharon (*mouthing*) I've got no knickers on.
Glynis (*loudly*) What?
Sharon (*in a louder whisper*) I've got no knickers on.

Leslie's and Terry's faces display their interest. Leslie having wriggled out of his underpants, is having difficulty getting first one foot then the other into his bathers as his towel is wrapped too tightly round him. Sharon, who in her endeavours, now has one foot caught in her trousers, hops backwards to release it. She encounters Leslie's roving hand. He gooses her

Leslie Wey-hey!

Sharon screams and staggers forward. Leslie grins. Shirley collapses her deck-chair and as she steps back, collides with Martin who is bending in his undressing efforts. Martin, who is clutching his towel, is shot forward on to his face

Glynis Martin!
Martin Sorry, dear. (*Holding his towel round his waist, he goes to her aid, holding her towel round her*)

Martin has one towel round his waist and is holding Glynis's round her, his bathers still at half mast. His towel, however, is insecurely knotted and slowly falls to the ground. He quickly flips half of the towel he is holding round Glynis round himself. That towel now does a semi-effectual job for them both as Glynis, who has already had trouble with buttons or poppers on her dress, has further trouble getting out of that, and getting her head through the halter of her one-piece swimsuit. Leslie, now in his bathing-costume, tries a couple of body-building poses sucking in his stomach impressively. It becomes too much for him and he lets it all go with a noise like a collapsing balloon. Shirley settles herself in her now righted deck-chair. Martin stretches out on his lilo, Leslie gets comfortable and Terry has got himself stretched out with a towel clutched in front of himself to hide any feelings he might have towards Sharon. Their attention is now drawn to Sharon who has got herself into the apparently insoluble position of having pulled on her tiny bikini bottoms over the towel she is holding round her waist. She pulls out the towel corner by corner and is finally in her bikini trunks. She turns to see, to her dismay, that everyone has been staring at her for some time. Embarrassed, she walks up her towel as she spreads it between Martin and Terry, stumbles to her place and sits hunched and embarrassed

Glynis Aren't you going to put your bikini top on, dear?
Sharon No, I don't think so.
Glynis Everyone else is.
Sharon Yeah.
Glynis Don't you want to get brown?
Sharon Not really, no.
Terry You said you was dying to get a tan on.
Sharon Well, I've changed me mind.
Glynis I'm sure Terry won't mind if you do, dear. He won't think you're forward. Will you, Terry?
Terry No.
Leslie Mind? He can't wait. Me neither. Come on, Sharon, give us all a treat. Show 'em off while they're peaches and cream. (*Resignedly*) They'll soon be prunes and custard.

Shirley Leslie, please.
Leslie If you're selling one of them puppies, I'll have the one with the pink nose.
Terry (*fiercely*) Shuddup.
Leslie Oops, sorry.
Shirley Leave them alone, Leslie.
Leslie I haven't touched 'em.
Shirley I mean Sharon and Terry.
Leslie So do I.

They both realize what they have said, and giggle

Sharon I'm going for a walk.
Terry I'll come, too.
Leslie I'm sorry, Sharon, I didn't mean nothing.
Sharon It's all right.
Shirley Take no notice of him, Sharon.
Sharon 'S all right, Mrs Thompson, I don't mind, honest. I'm used to it. I just want to explore a bit. You know. Look for fossils and things.
Leslie No offence I hope.
Sharon No, course not.
Glynis That's right, Sharon. You and Terry have a good explore. You don't want to sit with us old things.
Sharon (*to Terry*) All that old grey flesh. Makes me sick.

Terry and Sharon exit

Leslie Old grey . . .?
Shirley That's very naughty, Leslie. You've upset her properly.
Leslie I was only having a bit of fun.
Shirley I know that, dear, but not everybody's liberated like us.
Leslie Don't I know it.
Shirley She's only young, you know. And probably self-conscious.
Glynis Yes, she's aware, you see. Very aware. I blame the media. I mean girls are taught to be aware nowadays aren't they. Not like us.
Leslie Well, she'd have to be half-witted not to be aware of that pair.
Martin You've done it again.
Leslie What.

Martin Aware of that pair.

Glynis Martin.

Martin Sorry.

Glynis Yes, but things are different now to what they were.

Leslie Well, I dunno. When we was young a lovely pair was still a lovely pair. Look at Jane Russell—mean, moody and magnificent.

Martin That makes three.

Glynis glares

Shirley Course the pill does it, too, dunnit. Makes 'em bigger.

Glynis Oh, Sharon's not on the pill.

Shirley Really? That's a bit dangerous, innit?

Glynis No, she's never needed it. She's very—well, I know it's unusual these days but she's still—(*mouthing*)—*virgo intacta*.

Shirley Really?

Glynis Oh yes. I insisted.

Shirley Fancy, an attractive girl like Sharon doesn't take the pill.

Martin (*half hearing*) Yes she does.

Glynis Pardon.

Martin Yes, you made her, don't you remember? After that business with your brother's boy staying . . . (*His voice falters before his wife's glare*) No—no—that was—um—cod liver oil pills, wannit. Took 'em for—the vitamins—I mean—er—yes. (*He subsides*)

Shirley (*cosily*) Well, anyway she's a lovely shape, pill or no pill.

Glynis Of course she gets 'em from me, you know.

Martin (*with a faint flicker*) And my sister Joyce. She was very well-endowed.

Glynis I'm talking about quality, not quantity.

Martin fades completely

The sad thing is, when you're a young girl you never have a chance to enjoy 'em. You've only just got over the shock of getting 'em, when . . .

Leslie Flergh.

Glynis Quite. We're not taught to use our assets, are we. (*She looks at Martin*) God knows, I wasted mine. Threw 'em away.

Shirley What about her young man?

Glynis What about him?

Shirley I mean, he seems—very nice—I mean, is he . . . ?
Glynis Serious?
Shirley Yes, I mean, what's he do?
Glynis He's in his father's business.
Shirley Oh? His father's business. What's that, then?
Glynis Well, it may sound common, but it's very lucrative.
Shirley Oh, yes?
Glynis And expanding.
Shirley Oo-oh.
Glynis Not that that matters of course. It's Sharon's happiness.
Shirley Oh, yes. Of course.
Glynis As long as she loves him.
Shirley And he loves her.
Glynis Oh, he's besotted. Infactuated.
Shirley Well he would be.
Leslie So what's the business?
Glynis Well, it's retail. Pre-cooked sea foods and accessories.

Pause. Shirley, Martin and Leslie all react, puzzled

Martin It's a fish and chip shop.
Glynis *Three* fish and chip shops.
Shirley Oo.
Glynis And expanding.
Shirley I say.
Glynis And scampi. And chickens in baskets. Terry's father's very go ahead. He's starting escargots next year. And—(*she whispers*)—he's *not that well.*
Shirley Really?
Glynis He'll be obliged to loosen the reins, 'cos he can't keep it up. And when Terry gets it there'll be no stopping him. He's been studying. He's going to start a betting-shop. Then a chain of 'em. He'll be wealthy—almost rich.
Shirley Oo, I say.
Glynis Yes. He's a go-getter just like his dad. He'll go far.
Leslie I wonder how far he's going now.
Shirley Leslie!
Leslie *Now* what have I said?
Shirley Not everybody's like us, you know. (*To Glynis*) He forgets. I'm sorry. Just because we're—um—well because we've got no—I mean well when you're—liberated like us you forget

that not everybody is. Actually I'm not that liberated, really.
But *he* insists.

Leslie chuckles to himself

Glynis I'm sure I'm as liberated as the next.

Shirley Oh, yes. I didn't mean to say—but you got a daugher.
So you have to have different standards.

Glynis All I draw the line at is smut. (*Pause*) Smut and sex. (*Pause*)
And violence. (*Pause*) And grubby underwear.

Shirley distributes chicken legs and paper napkins

Leslie How about smoking?

Glynis No. I don't mind a smoke. In moderation. Oh, thank you.
But I can't stand Indian cooking and that man with no hair on
telly. I can't think what anyone sees in him. But I enjoy my
pleasures and I don't mind others enjoying theirs—providing.

Leslie Well, yes, I can see you're totally hip. What about Martin?
Is he liberated?

Martin Oh, yes, yes.

Leslie Do you like to indulge in a little wife-swapping?

Martin Eh?

Glynis Really.

Shirley Leslie.

Leslie It's all right. I wasn't gonna suggest nothing. (*To himself*)
Not bloody likely. Just getting to know Martin.

Martin (*considering*) It's always seemed to me that there's one
big disadvantage in wife-swapping.

Leslie What's that?

Martin It's only temporary.

There is a horrified pause

Glynis (*as last*) I beg your pardon.

Martin No, no, no. Nothing personal, dear. I'm speaking generally.

Glynis I should hope so.

Martin I mean you get used to one person, then you swap and
you gotta adjust. Then when you've adjusted yourself to the
channel where Angela Rippin's telling you what's what you
got to go back to Andrew Gardener. It's a nasty shock.

Leslie (*laughing*) Hallo, he thinks you look like Andrew Gardner.

Shirley Oh, Leslie really.

Leslie (*expansively*) It's all right. Glynis can take a joke, can't you, Glynis.

Glynis Oh, yes, yes.

Leslie There.

Glynis If it's funny.

Leslie reacts

Shirley See? He's always upsetting people. I just like to enjoy them. Even if they *are*—I mean I like to have a bit of company. Not drive 'em away. Live and let live. Be kind.

Martin Hear, hear.

Martin and Shirley smile warmly at each other

Leslie Oi-oi.

Shirley Oh, shut up. You upset everybody.

Leslie You mean I upset you.

Shirley Well, I'm used to you, but Martin and Glynis are new friends and possibly they aren't. Just be nice.

Leslie Aren't I always?

Shirley Well—yes, but well . . .

Leslie When haven't I been?

Shirley Well, I'm sure you know . . .

Leslie Oh, no, not that.

Shirley No, I never mentioned any particular.

Leslie Honestly.

Glynis What?

Shirley Nothing.

Glynis Oh.

Leslie All it was, was I had to make a speech at my brother's second wedding and I was taken ill.

Shirley No, no, no, I wasn't thinking of that. You couldn't help being taken poorly. It was just bad luck it went all over the wedding cake.

Leslie It was only spattered.

Shirley Well, it could happen to anyone I suppose, but none of your family's speaking now all the same.

Leslie When was you thinking of then.

Shirley Well—at Uncle Robert's funeral last month I thought you went a bit far. I mean I know my Cousin Esther is a bit strait-laced but——

Leslie Strait-laced? She could tie up Houdini!

Shirley Well you didn't have to say that about Uncle Robert.
He was a nice man.

Leslie Yeah, best of the lot of 'em.

Shirley Well, then.

Pause

Glynis Um—say what?

Shirley Nothing.

Glynis Oh.

Shirley I couldn't say.

Glynis Couldn't you try?

Leslie I will.

Shirley No, please. Well, Uncle Robert he—well—he lingered,
you know.

*At the word "lingered" the two women get stuck into a real natter
about illnesses. Leslie sighs and lies back*

Glynis Oh, dear. Yes. So did one of his lot. (*She nods at Martin*)

Shirley Yes, well. We was telephoned three times in seven weeks
to say he was sinking, and twice he floated up again.

Glynis Really.

Shirley Yes. He'd been on Benzedrine to pick him up, Mogadon
to knock him down, Cortezone, Methedrin and massive doses
of Aminophylline—taken suppositorially.

*Martin sadly lays aside the remainder of his chicken in mid-bite and
lies down*

Glynis Oh, I say.

Shirley But they never really knew what it was. They had head-
specialists—

*The two women continue almost in a liturgical chant, with Shirley
as priest and Glynis as the congregation*

Glynis —head-specialists—

Shirley —chest—

Glynis
Shirley } —specialists—(*Speaking together*)

Shirley —stomach—

Glynis
Shirley } —specialists—(*Speaking together*)

Shirley —and they said they knew—

Glynis ⎫
Shirley ⎭ —but they didn't. (*Speaking together*)

Glynis No, no, I know. Well, they have to pretend or they look such fools. What was it finally pulled him down?

Shirley It was the doings—

Even Glynis is puzzled at that

—finally—well, he struggled, but . . .

Glynis Yes, yes, I know. My grandmother was the same. They don't make 'em like that any more.

Shirley D'you know, his heart actually stopped once.

Glynis Did it.

Shirley Yes and they thumped him and he was off again.

Leslie Just like our boiler.

Shirley Anyway we was gathered for the last rites and the coffin was just on its runners going through the velvet curtain into the flame and—(*pointing to Leslie*)—he said "If Uncle Robert wakes up again now, sees them flames, then us lot he'll *know* where he is, won't he."

Glynis covers her laugh

Oh, I was so embarrassed. None of *that* side of the family are speaking to us now, either, it's always the same. Wherever we go. He makes life so lonely sometimes.

Pause

Martin Yes. I know what you mean.

Glynis gives him a look but he seems to be asleep

Shirley Oh, well, get some sun, I suppose. (*She lies back and closes her eyes*)

Glynis looks round at them, anxious to find an excuse to shatter the peace

Glynis Are you asleep Martin? (*Pause*) Are you asleep? (*Pause*) Martin, are you . . .

Leslie (*without moving*) Why don't you throw a bucket of water over him, then ask?

Glynis is still not satisfied

Glynis Martin, are you asleep?
Martin (*patiently*) No, just dreaming.
Glynis I was worried about Sharon. D'you think she's all right?
Martin D'you want me to go and find her?
Glynis No, no, it's all right. I think she can take care of herself.
  You have a nice rest.

Martin settles again at last, so does Glynis

  *Sharon and Terry run on, hand in hand, very happy. Sharon's
  bikini bottoms are on inside out. The label shows*

*They see the others are asleep then go into a kiss. Terry's hand
wanders to Sharon's bottom. He squeezes. There is a loud, drawn-
out, reverberating fart. Glynis rises to a sitting position, her appalled
face stares at the others. Terry and Sharon break and edge away
from each other looking round. Leslie sits up and sees that Glynis is
upright. He is amazed, but grins at her*

Leslie Coh, blimey, you're in fine voice today, aren't you.
Glynis *How dare you!*
Leslie Wasn't that you?
Glynis *How dare you!*
Leslie It came from your direction.
Glynis It came from yours!
Leslie No, no. Not my brand.
Glynis How *dare* you suggest it was me!
Leslie (*pointing up*) Well if it was that seagull he'd've come down
  in flames by now.
Glynis The *nerve*.

Shirley clutches at a straw

Shirley Perhaps it was the tide coming in.
Glynis (*waving her hat*) Tide? Tide? It was him trying to blame
  it on me.
Leslie Don't waft it over here.
Glynis I know your sort.
Leslie How about Martin. Martin? Martin, you crafty devil, was
  that you?

Martin dozes on

Glynis (*screaming*) Martin?! Martin! Was that you?
Martin Eh? What? Yes, dear?
Leslie (*quickly*) There you are.
Glynis Martin, really!
Martin Pardon?
Shirley No, it couldn't've been. Not Martin.
Glynis Oh, couldn't it. I know him.
Leslie Oi-oi. It's all coming out now.
Glynis Oh, shut up, you!
Martin I'm sorry, dear. Very sorry. What have I done?
Shirley There, see. It's not him.
Leslie He might've done it in his sleep.
Shirley Leslie, please.
Glynis You are disgusting.
Leslie What d'you mean, *I* am. It was *you* had two helpings of
  brussel sprouts last night.
Shirley Leslie.
Glynis Take him away from me. Take him away.
Martin I'm sorry, dear. Honest. I'd rather anything in the world
  had happened, but *what have I done*?
Leslie Farted.
Glynis Oh.
Martin No, no. Wasn't me. Honest.
Sharon Mummy. We're engaged.
Leslie Then it *was* Glynis.
Glynis I'll kill him! I know I will.
Sharon We're engaged, Mummy.
Leslie Hallo, was it one of you two?
Glynis I suppose that's what you call being liberated.
Terry Well, it wasn't me, but I heard it.
Leslie I should hope so. If you didn't hear that one you'd need
  a deaf-aid.
Glynis He's not fit to be seen with.
Shirley Oh, he's not that bad.
Glynis He is. He is.
Martin I swear, dearest, on my knees. I swear it wasn't me.
Sharon *Mum. Dad. I'm engaged.* To Terry. We're going to be
  married.
Glynis Oh, *well done*, dear.
Terry Eh?

Glynis I mean, congratulations—no—oh, I'm so happy for you both. I don't know what I'm saying.

Glynis embraces Sharon

Shirley There, look, they're engaged everybody. Isn't it wonderful. I'm so excited.

Sharon So am I.

Leslie Maybe that's what caused the . . . (*He blows a raspberry*)

Glynis shrieks

Shirley Well, isn't it lovely. How did it happen?

Terry I don't know, really. We went for a walk in the dunes and I just found myself saying it.

Martin, then Shirley, embrace Sharon

Martin Yes, it was the same with me.

Leslie Hallo, what you got on your back, Sharon?

Sharon Eh?

Leslie You're all covered in sand and bits. No wonder he didn't know what was happening to him.

Sharon What d'you mean?

Leslie You got your bikini bottoms on inside out.

Sharon Eh?

Leslie (*to Terry*) You young devil, you.

Sharon I must've done that when I was changing here.

Leslie Her-her. You been sampling the horses doovrays before the vicar's said grace?

Glynis Somebody stop him.

Shirley Leslie!

Leslie What you shouting at me for? Look at him. He's got sand on his knees, I'm just lying here minding me own business. There's these two going up and down like a fiddler's elbow, there's Glynis here doesn't know if she wants a doctor or a tyre change and you're all shouting at *me*.

Glynis (*shrieking*) Ah, Terry. Are you going to let him talk like that about your fiancée?

Terry I don't think you should talk like that about my fiancée.

Leslie Oh, knackers.

Glynis Martin, do something.

Martin Yes, dear. What?

Glynis It's always the same. Every crisis. *I* must face it.

In her rage, Glynis walks round in a circle, followed by Martin.
Every time they pass the surfboard they tread on it and it tips up

Martin Well, calm down, dear. You'll only bring on your back.
   I'm sure it's all for the best.
Glynis All for the best. All for the best. He's non compos.
Martin Just don't upset yourself, dear.
Shirley No. *He* can't help it.
Glynis That's right, you stick up for him.
Shirley Well he won't stick up for himself. Poor little thing.
Martin I'm not a poor little thing.
Leslie Don't you shout at my wife.
Glynis Don't you tell my husband who he can shout at.

Glynis's back goes. She grimaces in pain, holding it

Martin I wasn't shouting at her. I like her.
Shirley No, he wasn't.
Martin I just understand Glynis. She's highly strung.
Leslie (*triumphantly*) *That's* what caused it.
Glynis Martin, Terry. *Hit* him.

Terry	Well, I don't think I should . . .	
Glynis	Do something, one of you before I . . .	
Sharon	Go on, Terry, he's only little . . .	(*Shouting*
Shirley	I don't think you ought to incite . . .	*together*)
Leslie	Come on then. Both of you. One hand behind me back.	

Martin Oh, *shut up! Shut up! The lot of you!*

Glynis collapses on to the end of her chaise which folds up round her.
At last there is silence. A smile spreads over Martin's face at his
new-found power

   There, that's better.
Glynis He's never spoken to me like that before.
Shirley (*smiling*) Well, he has now.
Martin Look on the bright side, Glynis. The sun's shining. We're
   on holiday. And you've got what you wanted. You've made a
   wonderful bargain. The best superstructure in Stepney for
   three fish-and-chip shops. If she didn't have your sister Mar-
   garet's face she might have got MacFisheries but she's done
   very well.

Terry Here what d'you mean?

Martin And so have you, so relax. Sharon's an hard worker and there's plenty of fun in her. So just do what *I didn't*, keep her away from her mother, and give her one round the chops when she steps out of line and you'll both be very happy.

Sharon (*crying*) Oh, Dad.

Martin I'm talking for your good, too, so dry up and shut up.

Sharon Oh, Dad. (*She sobs*)

Terry comforts her

Glynis Now look what you've done. You've made her cry.

Martin She'll get over it.

Glynis Anyway what do you mean inciting Terry to hit her? Is that a way for a father to go on?

Martin Yes.

Glynis staggers to her feet

Glynis I'd like to have seen you ever lift a finger against me.

Martin Perhaps I should have.

Glynis Should have? Should have? If wishes were bunches of grapes we'd all be knee-deep in Beaujolais.

Shirley Oh, well, Glynis. Let's be happy. This is the happiest moment of your daughter's life.

Sharon sobs

Leslie Yeah, cheer up, Glynis. You'll soon be a mother-in-law.

Glynis Oh, shut up, you.

Leslie Coh, blimey. I was trying to be nice.

Glynis Nice? Nice? You should've thought of that just now . . .

Martin Now, *shut up*!

Martin jams a plastic bag down over Glynis's head. There is a moment's appalled silence

Leslie (*eventually*) If you really want to keep her quiet, don't forget the other end. (*He holds up the cork from the wine bottle*)

Glynis shrieks and pulls off the bag

Shirley Now, Leslie, really.

Glynis Let me get at him! Let me get at him!

Glynis starts hitting Leslie with her handbag

Leslie Help, help!

Leslie is on the ground. Glynis kicks his behind. There is pande-monium

    Oi, fight fair, can't you?

Glynis Fair, fair! I'll tear him to pieces!

Sharon Mum, Mum, mind your back.

Glynis *Sod* me back, I'll kill the bleeder!

Leslie Don't get personal.

Terry Mrs Spicer, Mrs Spicer.

Glynis Stand still and let me hit you.

Leslie Not bloody likely.

Glynis chases Leslie off. Terry and Sharon hurry after them, shouting

Shirley and Martin are left. Pause

Martin Coh, blessed peace.

Shirley Yeah, innit lovely.

Martin D'you think I should go and help him.

Shirley No, she'll never catch him in those shoes. You'll be for it when she comes back. Putting that bag over her head.

Martin I don't know why I never thought of it before. I do it to the budgie every night and he always shuts up.

They smile

    Funny how we go wrong in life, innit. One simple action could change everything.

Shirley Well, maybe. I wonder if Sharon and Terry are doing it right.

Martin They'll find out. Just because we did it wrong doesn't mean they have.

Shirley No. Hope springs eternal.

Martin You're so nice. So nice and—gentle.

Shirley Not as gentle as you.

Martin Eh?

Shirley Well. Generally I mean.

They smile

Martin You know what your Leslie said about wife-swapping!

Shirley Yeah.

Martin Well—now that Sharon'll be leaving home—well . . .
Shirley Well, I agree with you. I don't think I'd want to swap
  back.
Martin Well, we won't then.

*He shyly takes her hand. They both look out front, smiling con-
tentedly*

Shirley D'you think Glynis and Leslie'll be happy together?
Martin Provided they lay off the sprouts.
Shirley It's a beautiful place here, isn't it?
Martin Paradise. Let's come every year.

  Terry, Sharon, Glynis and Leslie come tearing back

Terry The tide's come in. All round us. We're cut off!
Leslie Help! Help! I can't swim.
Glynis Good. You'll drown first.
Sharon I can lie on me back and float.
Leslie Can I cling on to one?
Glynis (*hitting him*) He never stops, does he.

  Glynis chases Leslie off

Terry Come on, let's try this way.

  Terry and Sharon hurry off another way

Martin Can you swim?
Shirley Yeah, like a fish.
Martin Me, too. I was platoon champion.
Shirley D'you fancy some wine.
Martin Yeah, let's get plastered.

Shirley holds up the wine. They start to kiss as—

                    the CURTAIN *falls*

FURNITURE AND PROPERTY LIST

On stage: Sand
Large seaside postcard as backing

Off stage: Handbag, camera **(Sharon)**
Plastic carrier-bag. *In it:* towel, bikini bottom, copy of *Honey*, paperback **(Sharon)**
2 surfboards, 2 pairs of flippers, snorkel, 2 Jakari bats, duffel-bag with towel and trunks **(Terry)**
Deck-chair **(Shirley)**
Plastic carrier-bag. *In it:* bathing-cap, swimsuit, towel **(Shirley)**
Plastic carrier-bag. *In it:* trunks, towel, copy of *Men Only* **(Shirley)**
Cold bag. *In it:* 2 cans of beer—1 lager, 1 light ale, 1 bottle of Spanish Sauterne, corkscrew **(Shirley)**
Plastic bag. *In it:* stove, kettle **(Shirley)**
Straw bag. *In it:* thermos, cognac, cherry brandy, 4 paper napkins, bundle, 2 plastic glasses, plastic box with 4 pieces of chicken, plastic tablecloth **(Shirley)**
Lilo, lounger, beach ball, trunks, 2 towels, swimsuit **(Martin)**
Plastic carrier-bag. *In it:* box of tissues, copy of *Family Circle* **(Martin)**
3 carrier-bags stuffed with dressing **(Martin)**
Child's spade, roll of toilet paper **(Leslie)**
Binoculars **(Man)**

Personal: **Girl:** towel
Shirley: handbag
Terry: watch

LIGHTING PLOT

Property fittings required: nil
Exterior. A beach

To open: General effect of warm sunshine
No cues

EFFECTS PLOT

Cue 1	As CURTAIN rises *Seaside sounds—lighthouse foghorn, seagulls, waves,* *distant shouts*	(Page 1)
Cue 2	**Man** groans *Foghorn blast*	(Page 1)
Cue 3	**Man** squeaks with pleasure *Seagull squawk*	(Page 1)
Cue 4	**Girl** lies full-length on beach *Sound of seagull swooping and squawking*	(Page 1)
Cue 5	**Terry**: squeezes **Sharon's** bottom *"Loud, long, melodious fart"*	(Page 22)

MADE AND PRINTED IN GREAT BRITAIN BY
LATIMER TREND & COMPANY LTD PLYMOUTH

MADE IN ENGLAND